How to Evaluate
Past Performance:
A Best-Value Approach

The Monograph Series, 2d.

How to Evaluate
Past Performance:
A Best-Value Approach

SECOND EDITION

Vernon J. Edwards

NATIONAL LAW CENTER

GOVERNMENT CONTRACTS PROGRAM

Other titles in The Monograph Series, 2d.

Contractual Remedies for Product Substitution in Government Contracts
Peter D.P. Vint. 1994.

Overriding a CICA Stay
Timothy J. Saviano. 1995.

> This publication is designed to provide accurate and authoritative information in regard to the subject matter covered. It is sold with the understanding that the publisher is not engaged in rendering legal, accounting, or other professional service. If legal advice or other expert assistance is required, the services of a competent professional person should be sought.
>
> — From the *Declaration of Principles* jointly adopted by a Committee of the American Bar Association and a Committee of Publishers and Associations.

This book does not represent an official position of the U.S. Government or any U.S. Government agency.

ISBN 0-935165-35-5

ABOUT THE AUTHOR

Vernon J. Edwards is a lecturer at The George Washington University School of Business and Public Management Continuing Education Program in Contracting Services. Mr. Edwards is also a senior member of the professional staff of Educational Services Institute (Arlington, Virginia). He is a researcher, writer, and lecturer in the fields of Government contracting and project management. He has written many texts on the Government contracting process, including *Subcontracting Under the Federal Acquisition Regulation: A Primer* (George Washington University, 1993) and *Questions & Answers about Best-Value Source Selection* (George Washington, 1993).

Mr. Edwards has held several positions with the Federal Government, including Chief of Construction Contracting, Bonneville Power Administration, U.S. Department of Energy; member of the Contract Review Committee, HQ Air Force Systems Command; Tri-Services Contracting Officer; Contracting Officer, U.S. Air Force Space Division; and Director of Base Contracts, Los Angeles Air Force Base. He is a graduate of the University of California at Los Angeles.

CONTENTS

FOREWORD

The first edition of this monograph was published in June 1994. Since that time the final rule was published in May 1995. Although the evaluation of past performance is considered a "hot topic" in procurement, neither the Office of Federal Procurement Policy's Policy Letter 92-5 nor FAR 15.605 provide any practical guidance. This monograph provides practical "how to" guidance and also introduces a concept called Level of Confidence Assessment Rating (LOCAR), which the author defines as a numerical or verbal expression of the Government's degree of belief that an offeror is able and willing to keep its promises. The monograph emphasizes offerors' reputations for past performance as the key element in developing a LOCAR; however, the author notes that other factors could be used as well, such as qualifications of key personnel and subcontractors, the condition and capacity of facilities and equipment, and financial condition. Once a LOCAR is developed it is used to adjust the Government's preliminary evaluation of what offerors promise to do or deliver to arrive at a final evaluation of the "true" worth of those promises. In addition to this concept, the author wrestles with the difficult tasks of how to deal with the new offeror with no history of past performance, how to research offerors' past performance, and how to document evaluation results and conduct discussions.

Karen R. O'Brien
Director of Publications, Government Contracts Program

ACKNOWLEDGEMENTS

Thanks to my friends Ralph and Gwen Nash for their many kindnesses — the long and engaging conversations, the great dinners, and the wonderful times at Swan Point on those weekends when I had to be away from my family. I would also especially like to thank Karen O'Brien, Director of Publications for the Government Contracts Program, for her patience and support and for our long discussions in which the ideas in this monograph were worked out and refined. Her ideas, comments, arguments, and recommendations for changes to the text greatly improved this work and are very much a part of it. It is not too much to say that this text would not have been completed without her help.

Finally, love, thanks and praise to the team at home base — Carol, Joe, and Tom. Without them, nothing is possible.

HOW TO EVALUATE PAST PERFORMANCE:
A BEST-VALUE APPROACH

I. INTRODUCTION

On March 31, 1995, the General Services Administration, the National Aeronautics and Space Administration, and the Department of Defense issued Federal Acquisition Circular (FAC) 90-26, which revised the Federal Acquisition Regulation (FAR) to require, among other things, that federal agencies evaluate past performance in all competitively negotiated acquisitions that are expected to exceed $100,000.[1] This requirement is to be implemented in three phases, applying to solicitations expected to exceed $1,000,000 on or after July 1, 1995; solicitations expected to exceed $500,000 on or after July 1, 1997; and solicitations expected to exceed $100,000 on or after January 1, 1999.

The issuance of this final rule concluded a policy discussion begun in 1990 with the publication of *Procurement and Public Management: The Fear of Discretion and the Quality of Government Performance*, in which Professor Steven Kelman of Harvard University urged that Government agencies evaluate prospective contractors' past performance during source selection.[2] The discussion continued through the development of the Office of Federal Procurement Policy's (OFPP) Policy Letter No. 92-5 in late 1992 and its publication in January 1993.[3] The discussion then led to the February 1994 publication of a proposed rule to revise the FAR, the October 1994 passage of The Federal Acquisition Streamlining Act,[4] and the final rule. Thus, after nearly five years of discussion and debate, past

---

[1] 60 Fed. Reg. 16718 (May 30, 1995).

[2] Washington, D.C., The AEI Press (1990).

[3] 58 Fed. Reg. 3573 (Jan. 11, 1993).

[4] Pub. L. No. 103-355 (Oct. 13, 1994).

performance became a mandatory source selection evaluation factor for agencies of the Federal Government.

Using past performance as an evaluation factor in source selection is not a new idea, and federal agencies have done so since at least the early 1960s. The Department of Defense (DOD) established a formal contractor performance evaluation program in mid-1963.[5] Among the objectives of the program was the following:

> To furnish a long-term incentive to contractors by creating within the Government a "memory" of their performance and a means for considering this record in future actions relating to:
>
>   a. Source Selections
>   b. Determination of profit and fee
>   c. Renegotiation[6]

DOD's program directive required the submission of periodic reports of contractor performance and the establishment of a database[7] that was then used by DOD and NASA.[8] According to one report, this system was one of at least twenty-eight in existence at that time within the Department of

---

[5] DOD Directive 5126.38, "Program of Contractor Performance Evaluation," Aug. 1, 1963. For a discussion on the establishment of the DOD contractor evaluation program, see John A. O'Leary, *CPE and its Uses: A Dissertation*, 6 YPA 405 (1969). *See generally Report to the President on Government Contracting*, The Bell Commission, Apr. 30, 1962. The Bell Commission recognized that there was a need for "more exchange of information between agencies on their practices in contractor evaluation and on their experience with these practices."

[6] O'Leary, *supra* note 5, p. 410.

[7] *Id.* Under this system there were seven individuals forms, e.g., schedule performance and technical performance. A final report was included in the database and included an evaluation of total performance over the life of the contract. The final report remained in the database for seven years.

[8] *Id.*

Defense,[9] others being maintained by the Air Force System Command,[10] the Naval Ship Systems Command,[11] and the Secretary of the Army. At least one prime contractor, McDonnell Douglas Astronautics Company, hired a consultant to use the DOD system to evaluate its own programs; the company was so impressed with the results that it adopted the system as an internal management tool to evaluate the performance of subcontractors.[12] Hughes Aircraft Company also adopted the system for use in internal management.[13] The system eventually languished within DOD.[14]

The 1990s are witnessing renewed interest in the evaluation of past performance in the source selection process. However, neither the policy letter nor the FAR rule provides any practical guidance on how to evaluate past performance.[15]

---

[9] *Id.*, p. 414.

[10] AFSCR 70-7, AFSC R&D Contractor Performance Evaluation Reports.

[11] NAVSHIPS Manual 0900-000-3010.

[12] O'Leary, *supra* note 5, pp. 421-22.

[13] *Id.*

[14] The requirement of ASPR 1-908.3 for a Contractor Performance Record and the DD Form 1661 were deleted Nov. 30, 1971. See the notes to Revision 10 to Armed Services Procurement Regulation, Nov. 30, 1971, explaining that "[t]he benefits derived from CPR were not sufficient to warrant the cost involved."

[15] FAR 15.605, paragraph (b), reads as follows:

(b)(1) The evaluation factors that apply to an acquisition and the relative importance of those factors are within the broad discretion of agency acquisition officials except that —

(i) Price or cost to the Government shall be included as an evaluation factor in every source selection.

(ii) Past performance shall be evaluated in all competitively negotiated acquisitions expected to exceed $100,000 not later than January 1, 1999, unless the contracting officer documents in the

4   HOW TO EVALUATE PAST PERFORMANCE

Managers of commercial purchasing organizations have long recognized the importance of evaluating the past performance of vendor candidates, and most purchasing textbooks include descriptions of vendor performance rating systems.[16] There are, however, many differences between the work of commercial purchasing managers and the work of Government contracting officials, despite superficial similarities.   Government procurement regulations afford contracting officials less discretion than commercial purchasing managers enjoy.   Moreover, the Government's policies about competition in procurement and the existence of protest forums have made the Government's source selection process much more formal and complex than source selection in the commercial sector.

Most authors of textbooks and articles about vendor selection in the commercial sector have mainly addressed the repetitive purchase of large quantities of manufactured goods over extended periods of time.   There are

---

contract file the reasons why past performance should not be evaluated. Agencies may develop their own phase-in schedule for past performance evaluations which meets or exceeds the following milestones: All solicitations with an estimated value in excess of (A) $1,000,000 issued on or after July 1, 1995; (B) $500,000 issued on or after July 1, 1997; and (C) $100,000 issued on or after January 1, 1999. Past performance may be evaluated in competitively negotiated acquisitions estimated at $100,000 or less at the discretion of the contracting officer.

(iii) Quality shall be addressed in every source selection through inclusion in one or more of the non-cost evaluation factors, such as past performance, technical excellence, management capability, personnel qualifications, prior experience, and schedule compliance.

(iv) Environmental objectives, such as promoting waste reduction, source reduction, energy efficiency, and maximum practicable recovered material content (see part 23), shall also be considered in every source selection, where appropriate.

(2) Any other relevant factors, such as cost realism, may also be included.

[16] *See* Michiel R. Leenders et al., *Purchasing and Materials Management* (9th ed., 1993); Donald W. Dobler et al., *Purchasing and Materials Management Text and Cases* (5th ed., 1990); and *Procurement Quality Control* (James L. Bossert ed., 4th ed., 1988).

objective measures of past performance for such purchases, e.g., percent of defective shipments and number of late deliveries. However, 50 percent of all Government procurement expenditures are for services, for which objective measures of performance are more difficult to establish.[17] Also, Government agencies make many unique, one-time purchases for which they keep no records of contractor performance.

This monograph takes the position that the Government should use observations about an offeror's past performance to adjust the evaluation of an offeror to reflect the Government's level of confidence that the offeror will keep its promises. The specific procedure calls for the development of a Level of Confidence Assessment Rating (LOCAR), a numerical or verbal expression of the Government's degree of belief that an offeror is able and willing to keep its promises. This approach is consistent with the OFPP policy that past performance is to be used as a risk assessment factor.

Although this monograph emphasizes offerors' reputations for past performance as the key element in developing a LOCAR, other factors could be used as well, such as the qualifications of key personnel and subcontractors, the condition and capacity of facilities and equipment, financial condition, and any other information relevant to assessing the probability that an offeror will keep its promises. The LOCAR should be used to adjust the Government's preliminary evaluation of what offerors promise to do or deliver to arrive at a final evaluation of the "true" worth of those promises. The final evaluation — the determination of expected value — is what the Government should use to assess the relative value of competitive proposals and make the source selection decision.

The following section entitled "Source Selection Fundamentals" describes the Government's objectives in source selection and explains the concept of decisional rules. It also includes an overview of the steps in the source selection process and a description of evaluation procedures. Sections III through VIII describe a method for evaluating past performance. The last section includes closing comments. Readers already familiar with the source

---

[17] Federal Procurement Data System, *Federal Procurement Report: Fiscal Year 1992 through Fourth Quarter* (prepared by U.S. General Services Administration, 1992).

selection process can go directly to Section III. For an in-depth legal analysis of the source selection process, see Ralph C. Nash, Jr. & John Cibinic, Jr., *Competitive Negotiation: The Source Selection Process* (1993).

II. SOURCE SELECTION FUNDAMENTALS

A. Objectives of Source Selection

Source selection is the process of selecting a contractor and forming a contract. FAR 15.603 lists four objectives for this process:

(a) Maximize competition.

(b) Minimize the complexity of the solicitation, evaluation, and the selection decision.

(c) Ensure impartial and comprehensive evaluation of offeror's proposals.

(d) Ensure selection of the source whose proposal has the highest degree of realism and whose performance is expected to best meet stated Government requirements.

The last objective reflects the essential purpose of the source selection process — to select a reliable contractor and reach an agreement on contract terms and conditions. Essentially, the source selection process entails the following three steps:

(1) The Government solicits offers, called proposals. The Government's solicitation document, called a Request for Proposals (RFP), specifies the format for proposals, the Government's preferred terms and conditions, and the procedures for the conduct of the competition.

(2) Offerors prepare and submit proposals to the Government.

(3) The Government evaluates the proposals and accepts the one considered most advantageous to its interests based on criteria specified in the RFP.

B. Decisional Rules: Lowest-Priced-Technically-Acceptable and Best-Value Source Selection

In order to select a contractor, the Government must establish a rule that states the basis upon which it will decide which offer is most advantageous. Government agencies have traditionally used two decisional rules. The first rule calls for selection of the offeror whose proposal is technically acceptable and who offers the lowest price. This is called the "Lowest-Price-Technically-Acceptable" (LPTA) method of source selection. The second rule calls for selection of the offeror whose proposal reflects the best combination of features, whether or not the offeror's price is the lowest. This is called the "best-value" method of source selection.[18] The best-value method has been used for a long time and has become both increasingly popular and increasingly controversial in the late 1980s and early 1990s.

Every best-value source selection decision is based on a judgment as to which of the competing offerors has proposed the best combination of features. That judgment is made by an agency's source selection decision maker, commonly called the Source Selection Authority (SSA).[19] The SSA's best-value judgment must be based on information contained in the competing proposals and on other relevant information obtained by the agency, and must be consistent with the evaluation factors described in the agency's RFP.[20]

The Government's policy is to use information about an offeror's past performance when making source selection decisions.[21] This policy is based on the notion that an offeror's record of satisfying its customers in the past is indicative, though not necessarily determinative, of the likelihood that it will do so in the future. This notion is consistent with what ordinary experience teaches us about the behavior of people and organizations.

---

[18] FAR 15.602. The terms "lowest priced technically acceptable" and "best value" do not appear in the FAR but are generally accepted in actual practice.

[19] FAR 15.601.

[20] *See SIMCO, Inc.*, Comp. Gen. Dec. B-229964, 88-1 CPD ¶ 383.

[21] FAR 15.605(b).

C. Overview of the Source Selection Process

In a source selection, competing companies make promises (offers) to a Government agency. Whose promises should the Government accept? In a best-value source selection the questions that confront an agency are as follows:

(1) In what ways, if any, do the competitors' promises differ from one another? What are their relative strengths and weaknesses?

(2) If the promises reflect different strengths and weaknesses, then which of the promises has the most merit?

(3) Relatively speaking, how much confidence should the agency have in the ability and commitment of each of the competing companies to keep its promises?

(4) Taking into account both the relative merits of the promises and the relative reliability of each of the competing companies, which of the competing offers represents the best overall value to the Government?

The FAR provides no guidance on how to answer these questions, prescribing neither a detailed source selection process nor a proposal evaluation procedure.[22] However, by analyzing what agencies actually do, the phases of the source selection process become clear, each phase consisting of a series of tasks and products:

(1) **Presolicitation.** The Government plans the entire acquisition during the presolicitation phase, which can last for weeks, months, or even years.[23] Two important products of this phase are the acquisition plan

---

[22] *See* FAR Subpart 15.6.

[23] *See SMS Data Prods. Group, Inc.*, GSBCA 8589-P, 87-1 BCA ¶ 19,496, for a description of a procurement that took more than two years to complete.

and the source selection plan.[24] The source selection plan describes the evaluation factors for award and their relative importance, the evaluation process, and the structure of the evaluation organization.[25] The ultimate product of the presolicitation phase is the RFP, which includes a description of the product or services that the Government wants to buy, the terms and conditions that it would like to apply to the contract, and instructions to prospective offerors about how to compete for the contract.[26]

(2) Solicitation and Proposal Preparation. The public release of the RFP marks the beginning of the solicitation and proposal preparation phase, which often runs thirty to ninety days but can last longer in complex acquisitions. During this phase the Government may conduct a preproposal conference,[27] and usually publishes answers to questions received from prospective offerors. The Government may make "amendments" to the RFP and may extend the time for proposal preparation.[28] This is a period of intense activity on the part of the companies that decide to submit a proposal, and it ends with the submission of competing proposals by the deadline specified in the RFP.

(3) Initial Evaluation. The initial evaluation phase begins with the receipt of offers from prospective contractors. The Government usually convenes a panel to evaluate the proposals and to present its findings to a decision maker. The panel may include only a few members — five

---

[24] The requirement for agencies to do acquisition planning is at FAR 7.102. FAR 7.105 sets forth a general outline for a written acquisition plan. FAR 15.612(b)(3) requires that the source selection authority approve a source selection plan in formal source selections. The requirements for the content of the plan are at FAR 15.612(c).

[25] FAR 15.612(c).

[26] FAR Subpart 15.4.

[27] FAR 15.404.

[28] FAR 15.410.

or less — or it may include hundreds.[29] The panel is supervised by the agency's designated decision maker or SSA, usually the contracting officer, but in large acquisitions he or she may be a senior agency official.[30] The Government may take a few weeks or several months to evaluate proposals.[31] The main product of this phase is a report that describes the relative strengths and weaknesses of the competing proposals and that ranks the competitors from best to worst.[32]

Once the proposals have been evaluated, the Government must decide whether to make an award on the basis of the initial proposals, without discussions, or to establish a competitive range, conduct discussions, and solicit best and final offers (BAFOs) before determining which offeror proposes the best value. If the agency decides to award without discussions, the next phase is the contract award phase; otherwise, the discussion phase is next. The decision to make an award or to conduct discussions ends the initial evaluation phase.[33]

(4) Discussion. During the discussion phase the contracting officer notifies offerors who have been eliminated from the competitive range and conducts discussions with each of the offerors who have been determined to have a reasonable chance of winning the competition.[34] The contracting officer has considerable discretion in determining the format and content of the discussions, but he or she must point out the parts of each proposal which do not satisfy the Government's

---

[29] *TFX Contract Investigation Hearings Before the Senate Committee on Government Operations*, 89th Cong., 1st Sess. (1966). The source selection board had 200 members.

[30] FAR 15.612.

[31] *See SMS Data Prods. Group, Inc., supra* note 23.

[32] FAR 15.608.

[33] *See* Michael I. Mark, *Contract Award on Initial Proposals*, 19 PUB. CON. L.J. 252 (Winter 1990).

[34] FAR 15.609 and FAR 15.610.

requirements (called "deficiencies").[35]   The prospective offerors may revise their proposals during discussions, but when discussions have been concluded with all the offerors, the contracting officer must allow them to submit BAFOs.[36]   The objective is to receive as many acceptable BAFOs as possible so that the Government will have the widest range of choices. The call for BAFOs ends the discussion phase, which usually lasts only a few days but may occasionally extend to weeks or months.   The call for BAFOs will sometimes include amendments to the RFP.

(5) Best and Final Offer Preparation.   During this phase the competitors make final adjustments to their proposals. The Government sometimes allows competitors only a few days for this process. This is a critical phase, however, because most source selections include no more than one round of discussions. It is often an offeror's last chance to propose a winning deal and resolve any doubts the Government may harbor about its ability to do the job.

(6) Final Evaluation and Source Selection. The receipt of BAFOs marks the beginning of the final evaluation and source selection phase. The Government reconvenes the evaluation panel to make a final comparison of the competing offerors and to present the results to the contracting officer or SSA. Unless the evaluation factors were changed by RFP amendment, the evaluation panel uses the same factors to evaluate BAFOs that were used to evaluate the initial proposals.[37] The contracting officer or SSA then chooses the winner, normally basing his or her decision on the evaluation panel's findings. The decision maker is not, however, bound by the findings or recommendations of the evaluation panel and is free to make an independent assessment of the proposals.   The only constraints on the decision maker are the description of the evaluation factors for award in the RFP, the

---

[35] FAR 15.610(b).

[36] FAR 15.611.

[37] FAR 15.611(c).

description of their relative importance, and what the Comptroller General of the United States calls "the tests of rationality."[38]

(7) Contract Award. During the final phase of the source selection process, the contracting officer prepares the contract award file documentation and obtains any preaward clearances and approvals required by regulation and policy. Upon receipt of final approval to make the award, the contracting officer notifies the winner and the losers and distributes the contract document through official channels. Losers are entitled to a "debriefing" upon request.[39] Once the contracting officer has conducted any required debriefings, the process is ended, unless one or more companies protest the award, in which case the Government will have to suspend contract performance pending a protest decision[40] unless it receives an override.[41] If the Government wins the protest, the process is ended. If the Government loses, the next step is determined by the instructions received from the protest tribunal.

D. Evaluation Procedures

In order to select a contractor that offers best value, the Government should perform the following seven tasks:

(1) Select the evaluation criteria or "factors" that it will use to compare the competing offers.

(2) Establish the rule that states how it will use the factors to make the selection.

(3) Solicit offers.

---

[38] *Bank Street College of Education*, Comp. Gen. Dec. B-213209, 84-1 CPD ¶ 607.

[39] FAR 15.1001.

[40] FAR Part 33.

[41] For a discussion of CICA overrides, see Timothy J. Saviano, *Overriding a CICA Stay* (1995).

(4) Evaluate the competing offers and identify their relative values.

(5) Rate the relative capability and reliability of each of the competing offerors and develop a level of confidence (risk) assessment.

(6) Combine these findings into a determination of overall expected value for each offeror.

(7) Compare the overall expected values and identify the offeror that represents the best overall value.

1. Selecting the Evaluation Factors

The Government determines the value of offers on the basis of its evaluation factors for award (i.e., evaluation criteria). The selection of evaluation factors for award is a fateful matter for the Government for two reasons. First, the evaluation factors are a constraint on the Government's freedom to choose. The FAR states that the Government must evaluate the competing proposals solely on the basis of the evaluation factors described in the RFP and on their stated relative importance.[42] Second, the choice of evaluation factors determines, in large measure, the information the Government must seek from the competing offerors and the evaluation procedures that the evaluation panel must use. Indeed, it is probably not too extreme to say that most problems in source selection are ultimately related to the selection and description of evaluation factors for award. Nevertheless, the FAR provides very little guidance to Government officials about how to choose evaluation factors.

FAR 15.605(b) states that the choice of evaluation factors is within "the broad discretion" of agency officials. The subsection goes on to state that agencies must evaluate price or cost to the Government in every source selection; that they must evaluate past performance in every source selection expected to exceed $100,000; and that they must evaluate "quality" in every source selection through the inclusion of one or more "non-cost evaluation factors," citing "past performance, technical excellence, management capability, personnel qualifications, prior experience, and schedule

---

[42] FAR 15.608(a), FAR 15.611(d), and FAR 15.612(d).

compliance" as examples of such factors. FAR 15.605(d) requires that solicitations provide for selection of the competing offeror that offers the "greatest value" to the Government. It also requires that solicitations "state" the evaluation factors that an agency will consider when determining value and also state the relative importance of each of the factors. The FAR does not define the term "evaluation factors" other than in terms of the examples described above.

Evaluation factors are attributes of an offeror and of what the offeror promises to do or deliver in response to the terms and conditions of the solicitation. Attributes are features, qualities, and characteristics of the offeror as a firm and of its promised performance. It is these features, qualities, and characteristics that determine the value of a proposal. In the most frequently used model, the value of a proposal is the sum of the weighted values of the individual evaluation factors, as determined by the agency. In symbolic terms, value may be defined as follows, where w_i is the weight of factor x_i and $v_i(x_i)$ is the value associated with factor x_i:

$$v\,(proposal) = \sum_{i=0}^{n} w_i v_i(x_i)$$

Once an agency has determined the value of each proposal based on the stated evaluation factors, the agency must compare the values of the competing proposals to determine which has the greatest value.

In best-value source selection the Government expects that competing offerors will possess relevant attributes in different degrees. For instance, aspects of one offeror's product will be of better or worse quality than another's, or one offeror's price will be higher or lower than another's. A product may be more or less reliable, or a reputation for past performance may be more or less favorable. The Government also assumes that the value of a proposal will vary in relation to the degree to which it possesses the relevant attributes. Thus, a proposal's value is a function of its performance on the relevant attributes. When product reliability is an evaluation factor, a product that is more reliable than a competing product is more valuable than its competitor. The relationship between attribute performance and value is sometimes called a "value function," an idea illustrated in Figure 1 below.[43]

It is often true — though not necessarily true — that no single offeror will rank best on all factors when the Government applies more than one evaluation factor for award during proposal evaluation. In such cases, the Government will have to make tradeoffs, giving up some amount of one factor in order to get more of another, or accepting more of one factor in order to get more of another, or giving up some amount of one factor in order to avoid more of another. In fact, a best-value source selection is simply one in which the Government applies more than one evaluation factor for award during proposal evaluation and in which tradeoffs may be necessary.

The concept of making tradeoffs is at the heart of best-value source selection. The ultimate tradeoff, the one that the Government must explain and justify in the event of a protest, is the tradeoff between price and the other evaluation factors for award, sometimes referred to as the price or cost/technical tradeoff. This tradeoff entails deciding whether any marginal or management advantage that an offeror may have is worth any marginal difference in price. The FAR does not prescribe a tradeoff procedure, but many techniques are available.[44]

2. *Formulating the Decisional Rule*

In best-value source selection the decisional rule ought to state that the Government will award the contract to the offeror who represents the best

---

[43] Source of Figure 1 is Detlof von Winterfeldt and Ward Edwards, *Decision analysis and behavioral research* (1986) (quoting P. Gardiner, *The application of decision technology and Monte Carlo simulation to multiple objective public policy decision making: A case study in California coastal zone management* (1974) (unpublished Ph.D. dissertation, University of Southern California)).

[44] *See, e.g.*, Defense Systems Management College, *Systems Engineering Management Guide*, Chapter 8, Evaluation and Decision: Trade Studies (Superintendent of Documents, Washington, D.C. (1990)). For a complete description of a variety of techniques with theoretical explanations and extensive references, see von Winterfeldt and Edwards, *supra* note 43.

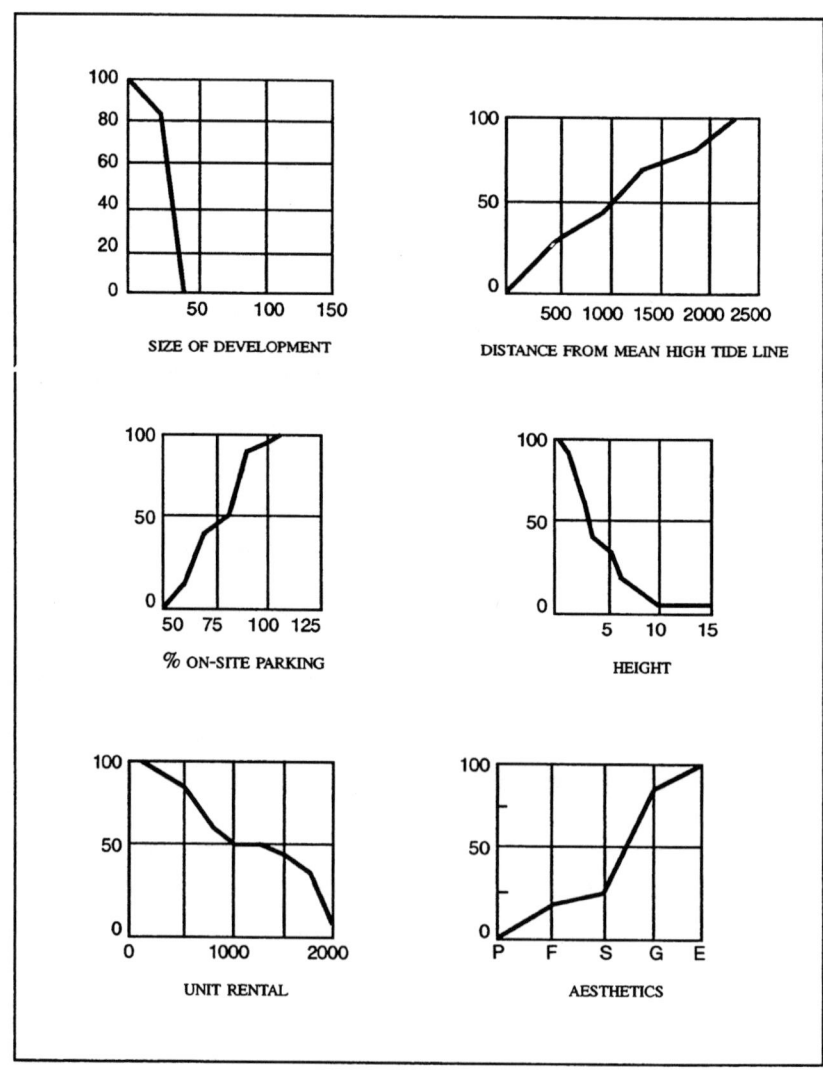

Figure 1. These "value functions" are examples of scoring rules that relate specific levels of factor performance to specific levels of value. They transform measurements and ratings on scales of diverse, incommensurable units into measurements on a common value scale. The transformed values can be aggregated into a single, overall expression of value. The application of importance weights will adjust the values to reflect the relative importance of the factors.

expected value. Each offer that the Government receives is a set of promises made by the offeror — essentially, promises to comply with the terms of the RFP if awarded the contract. When the Government evaluates these offers, it is evaluating promises. Thus, the Government's assessment of value is an assessment of promised value. The promised value is the sum, or integrated assessment, of the weighted values of the individual evaluation factors for award.

Once the Government has determined the promised value of each offer, it should ask itself whether or not it may safely rely on that offer. In other words, it should assess the risks associated with each offer and determine how much confidence to place in the offer. This determination should be based on an assessment of each offeror's ability and willingness to keep its promises.

The expected value of an offer is its promised value adjusted on the basis of the Government's level of confidence that the offeror will be able and willing to keep its promises. The idea behind expected value is that the Government should first determine the value of the offeror's promises, then determine the degree to which it may rely on those promises. The Government should make its source selection decision on the basis of an integrated assessment of those determinations. This decisional rule should be applied in every best-value source selection.

3. Soliciting Offers

The Government's third task is to solicit offers. In order to solicit offers the Government must prepare and issue an RFP. Most RFPs are prepared in the *Uniform Contract Format*, described in FAR 15.406. The *Uniform Contract Format* does not apply to all RFPs and contracts, but whether prepared in the *Uniform Contract Format* or not, all RFPs have two components: (1) a model contract and (2) a set of instructions and ground rules for the conduct of the competition. The model contract encompasses Sections A through K of the *Uniform Contract Format*. It is a complete set of contract terms and conditions — a specification or statement of work, a delivery schedule, and clauses. All that is missing are prices (or estimated costs and fees) for the work and the offeror's expression of assent to its terms.

Effectively, the RFP instructions tell the offerors to (1) read the model contract, (2) decide whether or not they are capable of performing the work, and (3) decide whether or not they are willing to perform the work in accordance with the terms and conditions in the RFP. The instructions tell prospective contractors that if they would like to make an offer in response to the RFP then they should propose prices (or estimate costs and propose fees), and complete the pricing schedule in Section B, the certifications and representations in Section K, and the appropriate information blocks on the RFP form, e.g., blocks 12 through 18 of Standard Form 33, Solicitation, Offer and Award. In short, the RFP not only solicits offers but also specifies the form and content of the offers. Thus, the most fundamental promise that an offeror is asked to make is the promise to accede to the terms and conditions of the RFP model contract and complete the specified work in accordance with those terms and conditions.

In addition to this fundamental promise, the RFP may require offerors to make supplementary promises, in the form of detailed descriptions of specific products or services that the offeror will supply or render. For example, if the RFP specification describes only a type of product, the RFP may instruct offerors to describe the specific make and model or design that they propose to furnish. Or, if the RFP statement of work describes a service in only general terms, the RFP may instruct offerors to describe the specific tasks they intend to perform or the specific procedures they intend to follow when rendering the service.

The RFP may allow offerors to submit alternative proposals. It may specify a supply or service in detail while allowing offerors to propose different products or services, or to bargain for different terms and conditions, or both. The FAR permits this in negotiated contracting if the Government is open to alternatives.[45]   In such a case, the RFP "requirements" are merely expressions of preference. The submission of an alternative proposal would not, in itself, render the proposal unacceptable.

---

[45] FAR 15.102 states that "bargaining is permitted."

4. Determining the Relative Merits of the Competing Offers

Once the Government has received offers in response to its RFP, its fourth task is to identify the relative strengths and weaknesses of each of the competing offers and make a determination of the relative value of each offer.[46] An offer is a promise or set of promises. Thus, the agency must determine what each offeror has promised. The kinds of promises that an offeror makes are largely determined by the RFP.

If, in response to an RFP, all competing offerors accede to the terms of the model contract, and if those terms are complete, then all offers will be identical — and of equal value — except for their prices and their organizational attributes. In other words, if the RFP is a complete and final expression of the Government's requirements — i.e., the specification or statement of work are "design" documents — and the RFP neither requires nor allows any supplemental or alternative technical response from an offeror, then the only basis for differentiating competing offerors will be their prices or estimated costs and fees and their capabilities and performance records.

If, for example, an RFP describes a specific make and model device that the Government wants to buy, then all that the Government should require from competing offerors is the promise to provide that make and model at a specified price. The Government should then select the acceptable offer with the lowest price.[47]

If the RFP specifies the product or service in detail, and neither requires nor permits supplemental or alternative proposals, then every offeror who promises to comply with the terms and conditions described in the RFP has offered something of equal value, and every offeror who proposes something

---

[46] FAR 15.608(a)(2).

[47] For references to functional, performance, and design specifications, see FAR 10.002(a)(4). For an analysis of the legal differences among the three types of specifications, see John Cibinic, Jr. and Ralph C. Nash, Jr., *Formation of Government Contracts* (1982; 2d ed., 1986), pp. 339-345.

different has made an unacceptable proposal. Thus, there is little point to having "technical" evaluation factors. Such factors make sense only when the offerors are expected or encouraged to propose different products or services and when the Government is willing to treat offerors more or less favorably on the basis of what they propose to do or deliver.

However, if the RFP describes only the basic functions that a commercial device must perform or the minimal levels of performance that it must achieve, then the RFP should instruct competing offerors to provide a technical proposal that describes the specific make and model to be delivered and information that will enable the Government to determine what functions the offered device will, in fact, perform and at what levels of performance. The Government must then compare the strengths and weaknesses of the competing offers and trade off the marginal differences in price to determine which is most advantageous overall. Unless the RFP states that the Government is seeking, and will give more favorable consideration to, additional functions and above-minimum levels of performance, the Government should treat all offers satisfying functional or performance requirements as equally valuable.

A well-written RFP states clearly the kinds of supplemental promises that the Government requires of offerors and the kinds of alternative promises the Government will entertain. If the Government neither requires supplemental promises nor agrees to entertain alternative proposals, then there is no need for a "technical" proposal. If, on the other hand, the Government requires supplemental promises to complete the expression of mutual assent that will be the basis for the contract, then the instructions for the preparation of technical proposals — the description of the kinds of information the offerors must submit — should be very precise.

Price or estimated cost and fee are part of the offer; they are something that the offeror is promising. The FAR requires that the Government always evaluate price or cost and fee.[48] Moreover, it is reasonable to expect that offerors will usually propose different prices or different estimated costs and proposed fees, and that the Government will give more favorable

---

[48] FAR 15.605(b).

consideration to reasonable, realistic prices or costs and fees that are lower than those proposed by competing offerors.

5. Rating Offerors' Capability and Reliability and Developing Level of Confidence Assessments

Once the Government has determined the relative value of an offer, it must decide how much confidence to place in those promises. The ultimate value of an offer depends not only on the merits of its promises but also on the ability and willingness of the offeror to keep those promises.

There are two steps in performing this task. First, the Government must consider all the evidence and rate each offeror on each of the factors that the Government has decided to use to develop its level of confidence assessment. Then the Government must consider those ratings and decide how much confidence to place in each offeror. The level of confidence may be expressed in descriptive terms or numerically. Descriptive expressions of confidence include words such as "high," "moderate," and "low." Numerical expressions of confidence should be made on a scale of 0 to 1, inclusive, with 0 indicating no confidence in an offeror's promises and 1 indicating complete confidence. A rating of .5 indicates that the Government thinks that the likelihood that the offeror will keep or fail to keep its promises is identical (i.e., 50/50).

On what basis should the Government determine the reliability of an offeror's promises? It is reasonable to expect that, apart from their offers, the offerors themselves will differ from one another in certain ways and that these differences can provide bases for competitive differentiation. The nature of the differences among competitors will depend on the factors of production or performance and their different company histories. Companies in a given industry that offer products or perform services that are close substitutes for one another will be more or less alike in many respects. Nevertheless, pertinent differences may exist in their capacities to perform and in their records of performance.

Government agencies have traditionally referred to the factors that relate to these kinds of differences among offerors as "management" factors.[49] Such factors have included aspects of an offeror's performance ability and capacity, such as the condition and capacity of facilities and equipment; the qualifications of key personnel; and cost, schedule, quality, and safety practices. They also include the offeror's record of performance. These factors say something about an offeror's ability and willingness to keep its promises. They are not things that are being offered to the Government per se. Rather, they are things that can be expected to shed light on the reliability of an offeror's promises. They provide a basis for making an assessment of the probability that an offeror will do what it has promised to do. They thus provide a basis for determining the risk associated with each offer.

Unfortunately, it has become common practice for Government agencies to ask offerors to prepare and submit performance plans as part of their proposals — e.g., management plans, quality assurance plans, cost/schedule control plans, and personnel recruitment plans. Offerors are commonly asked to "address every task in the statement of work and describe your approach to performing the task." "Soundness of approach" and similar evaluation factors are very popular. Such requirements and evaluation factors reflect the desire of Government agencies to develop some sense of the relative capabilities of competing offerors. A good plan or "approach" presumably reflects a knowledge of the nature of the work, from which it is inferred that the offeror is capable of doing the work and that its promises to do so can be afforded a higher degree of confidence than those whose plans are unsound.

Consider, for example, the following proposal preparation instruction from an Air Force RFP for the acquisition of technical support services:

> In the technical/management proposal, the Offeror shall provide the Government with information to clearly show the Offeror's soundness of approach and understanding of the requirement for the required technical support. The proposal must also contain a clear, concise description of how the Offeror plans to manage the efforts defined in the statement of work,

---

[49] Ralph C. Nash, Jr. and John Cibinic, Jr., *Competitive Negotiation: The Source Selection Process* (1993), pp. 141-144.

the quality of personnel that will perform the work effort, what resources and facilities will be used to perform or support these tasks, and how the transition from the current effort will be managed.

What kinds of responses might an agency receive to such an instruction? What kind of information would an offeror include? What would the information reveal about an offeror's ability?

A plan is a statement of intentions. Plans must be developed without perfect knowledge about the course of future events. No matter how many contingencies are envisioned, there is always the possibility that an unexpected event will cause the plan to go awry. Moreover, a well-designed and well-written plan may reflect only a proposal writer's talent rather than a company's ability to complete the work. Many people are capable of writing plans to do things they have never done, especially if given enough time to research the problem. Furthermore, effective analysis and evaluation of such documents depend on extensive experience with the work. If a person is evaluating a plan for something that he or she has never done, then his or her evaluation might have limited merit.

It is reasonable to believe that the most effective single predictor of future behavior is past behavior, even if one believes that the past does not determine the future. A Government agency can never know with complete certainty how a contractor will perform. However, the way that a contractor has performed in the past surely has some bearing on what can be expected of future performance. Thus, one way for the Government to reduce uncertainty about an offeror's future performance is to determine whether that offeror satisfied its customers in the past. It is reasonable to believe that if an offeror has consistently satisfied its customers in the past, then it is likely that the offeror will satisfy its customers in the future. (This, of course, assumes there have been no major changes in the company's condition or circumstances.) The idea of the predictive value of past performance is discussed in more detail in Section IV.

6. Combining Assessments of Promised Value with Levels of Confidence

Once the Government has evaluated each of the proposals and determined how much confidence to place in the offerors, it must combine those assessments to arrive at an estimate of the overall value of each offer. A numerical scoring example will illustrate this step. Suppose that a Government agency is buying a product and will use two sets of evaluation factors — technical and price. Suppose further that the Government will describe the results of its technical evaluation on a numerical scale of 0 to 100, with 100 being best. Suppose finally that the Government will express its level of confidence on a scale of 0 to 1, as described in the preceding subsection.

One offeror is given a technical score of 95. The Government's level of confidence in that offeror is set at .4, based on the offeror's performance record. On the basis of these assessments, the expected value of that proposal is 38 (95 x .4 = 38). In comparison, another offeror is given a technical score of only 86. However, the Government has greater confidence in this offeror and assesses its level of confidence at .9. This offeror's expected value is 77 (86 x .9 = 77). In this example, the first offeror makes better promises, but the Government has greater confidence in the second offeror, so the expected value of the second offeror's promises is greater.

In this example, a numerical system makes the determination of expected value relatively simple, but formal, since it is calculated arithmetically. If the Government used an adjectival system — with the promised value described as "excellent," "good," "fair," or "poor," and the level of confidence as "high," "moderate," or "low" — then the Government would have had to make an intuitive determination of expected value. There is no standard procedure for combining a rating of excellent with a low level of confidence ("excellent" x "low" = ?), although a set of rules could easily be established for that purpose.

In the numerical example above, the level of confidence assessment, based on the offerors' past performance record, was used to adjust the promised value of the proposals to determine their "true" or expected value. Past performance was therefore used as an adjustment factor, rather than as an attribute having inherent value per se. (A different approach for determining expected value would be to rate past performance, assign it a value based on the rating, and add that value to the values of the other factors.) The source selection decision should be based on the integrated assessment of expected value and price.

7. Comparing Offerors Based on Relative Expected Values

Once the Government determines each offeror's expected value, it must then compare the offerors to each other by ranking them from best to worst and determining which offeror has the highest expected value (best value). The Government's scoring system should facilitate this process by making initial comparisons as simple as possible (77 points versus 38 points in the example above is a relatively simple comparison to make).   But the Government's decision maker must base his or her ultimate best-value tradeoff decision on an analysis and comparison of the descriptions of the substantive differences among the competitors, i.e., their relative strengths, weaknesses, deficiencies, and risks, and not on scores per se.

III. WHAT IS PAST PERFORMANCE?

A. The Definition of Past Performance

What does an agency mean when it says that it is going to evaluate an offeror's past performance? What, exactly, is it going to evaluate? Is an offeror's past performance a set of facts about an offeror's past actions, or is it a set of opinions about those actions?

"Past performance" is a composite of three things: (1) observations of the historical facts of a company's work experience — what work it did, when and where it did it, whom it did it for, and what methods it used; (2) qualitative judgments about the breadth, depth, and relevance of that experience based on those observations; and (3) qualitative judgments about how well the company performed, also based on those observations. Some agencies have applied the term "experience" to the first two elements, and distinguished them from the third element, which they have called "past performance."[50] Thus, some agencies state in the RFP that both experience

---

[50] *See Source Evaluation Board Handbook,* Appendix I to NFS 18-70.303 § 303 (NHB 5103.6B, Oct. 1988).

and past performance will be evaluated as separate factors.[51]   However, these are just different aspects of the same set of observations. Moreover, a review of the Comptroller General's protest decisions reveals that not all agencies have made such a clear distinction, and that some have used the term "past performance" in a way that encompasses all three elements.[52]

The FAR does not define past performance per se, but defines "past performance information" as follows in FAR 42.1501:

> Past performance information is relevant information, for future source selection purposes, regarding a contractor's actions under previously awarded contracts. It includes, for example, the contractor's record of conforming to contract requirements and to standards of good workmanship; the contractor's record of forecasting and controlling costs; the contractor's adherence to contract schedules, including the administrative aspects of performance; the contractor's history of reasonable and cooperative behavior; and generally, the contractor's business-like concern for the interest of the customer.

Some commentators have argued that evaluations of past performance should be based entirely on objective facts and should not be based on opinions as to how well a company performed in the past.[53]   However, the only "facts" available to the Government are the observations of human beings, which will always include subjective elements. Thus, the evaluation of past performance has to include both objective determinations and

---

[51]   *See, for example, A. G. Crook Co.*, Comp. Gen. Dec. B-255230, 94-1 CPD ¶ 118 and *ISS Energy Servs., Inc.*, Comp. Gen. Dec. B-249323.3, 93-2 CPD ¶ 30.

[52]   For an analysis of the Comptroller General's protest decisions on past performance, see Carl J. Peckinpaugh, *Evaluations of Vendor Experience and Past Performance in Government Contracting Decisions*, 60 FCR 677 (Dec. 27, 1993).

[53]   Letter from Donald J. Kinlin, Chair, Section of Public Contract Law, American Bar Association to Charles W. Clark, Office of Federal Procurement Policy (Jan. 12, 1994) (on file at the Government Contracts Program of The George Washington University).

subjective assessments. Facts alone are not sufficient to enable an agency to evaluate a company's past performance.

For example, RFPs commonly ask offerors to provide information about recent contracts. Such RFPs often ask offerors to state for each contract performed the estimated cost or negotiated price of the contract, the actual cost or final price, and the negotiated delivery or completion date and the actual delivery or completion date. Suppose an offeror states that the estimated cost of a cost-reimbursement contract was $1,000,000 and that the actual cost was $1,700,000, a 70-percent cost overrun. Do these facts imply poor cost estimating or poor cost control? Suppose a contract specified a delivery date of 10 June 1989, but the contractor actually delivered on 17 September 1989. Do these facts imply poor schedule compliance? Most people would probably agree that these facts may indicate poor performance, but not necessarily. Many factors not attributable to poor contractor performance could account for these events. Thus, a contracting officer would want to investigate further before rendering a judgment.

While it is one thing to know factually what happened in a company's past — the who, what, when, where, and how — it is an entirely different issue to understand the meaning of such facts, since they took place within a context that may be difficult to reconstruct or understand. Most contract administrators would assert that a 70-percent cost overrun or a 78-day late delivery is bad. But what if the customer was very happy with the company's performance, stating that the contractor did a marvelous job under the circumstances? What if the customer further states that had it not been for the contractor's superior performance, the outcome would have been much worse? Thus, facts alone, without judgments, may be of limited use to agency evaluators.

Facts concerning past performance are often hard to obtain. Many organizations do not keep extensive files of factual information about contractor past performance. Some organizations record only their employees' judgments about how well or how poorly a contractor performed. Consider, for example, the Government's program for evaluating construction and architect-engineer contractors, prescribed in FAR 36.201 and FAR 36.604. The forms used to evaluate performance are Standard Form (SF) 1420 and SF 1421. SF 1420, Performance Evaluation—Construction Contracts, requires customers to evaluate five performance elements:

(1) quality of work, (2) timely performance, (3) effectiveness of management, (4) compliance with labor standards, and (5) compliance with safety standards. It further requires that customers assign the following three ratings to each performance element: outstanding, satisfactory, or unsatisfactory (SF 1421 uses excellent, average, and poor), but provides no criteria for making such assessments, with the result that they will be almost entirely subjective (but not necessarily arbitrary). The form asks the evaluator to provide facts in support of outstanding or unsatisfactory ratings "in sufficient detail" to be of assistance to persons using the form to review the qualifications of potential contractors. (SF 1421 asks only for "remarks.") Obviously, anyone who rates a contractor outstanding or unsatisfactory will marshal facts that will support that opinion. A close examination of SF 1420 and SF 1421 reveals that the amount of truly objective information on the forms — evaluator-independent information — is very limited. With few exceptions, the facts appearing on the form will support the performance evaluator's subjective assessment. Contractors that have been given unsatisfactory or poor ratings may submit comments, including facts chosen to support the contractor's contrary assessment of its performance. The evaluator must include these comments in the report.

In order to evaluate past performance an agency must obtain three kinds of information. First, the agency has to collect observations about what work a company did, when and where the work was done, how the work was done, and the customers for whom the work was done. Second, the agency has to make or obtain judgments about the breadth, depth, and relevance of the work performed. Third, the agency has to make or obtain judgments about the quality of that work — how well that work satisfied the customers for whom it was done.

The agency must use this past performance information to judge the overall quality of the company's past performance. The Government must be judicious and rational when making such assessments, carefully sifting and weighing all the available evidence on the basis of its age and relevance, the credibility of its sources, and the offeror's responses to unfavorable reports. The agency should look for indications of a pattern of either favorable or unfavorable overall performance, rather than focusing on individual successes or failures. It must then integrate that assessment with its assessments concerning any other factors that will affect its level of confidence, such as the qualifications of key personnel or the capacity of facilities and equipment.

An agency may have experience with an offeror and therefore have information in its own files about that offeror's past performance. If an agency does not have its own information, it must identify sources of information — persons who know something about the offeror's past performance. There are two types of sources of information. The first type provides information about an offeror's performance under specific contracts. These persons are usually employees of current or former customers of the offeror. The second type provides information of a more general nature. These persons include officials and employees of Government licensing and law enforcement agencies, credit reporting organizations, better business bureaus, industry associations, former subcontractors, and federal, state, and local courts.

B. Specific Areas of Inquiry

Because past performance may pertain to any number of things, it is helpful to break it down into more specific areas of inquiry. These specific areas of inquiry include:

(1) The nature and duration of the work and the conditions of performance;

(2) The quality of supplies delivered or services rendered, in terms of compliance with adequate specifications and statements of work;

(3) The timeliness of performance, taking into account all excusable delays;

(4) The cost or price of performance, in terms of initial reasonableness and control of exigencies (i.e., changes and claims);

(5) The offeror's reasonable compliance with other contract terms and conditions;

(6) The effectiveness of the offeror's management of the administrative aspects of performance, such as communicating and performing routine clerical tasks;

(7) The offeror's willingness to cooperate with, and assist, the customer in routine matters and when confronted by unexpected difficulties; and

(8) The offeror's business integrity.

These are basic inquiries that an agency should consider in every procurement in which past performance is an evaluation factor. An agency should also consider other applicable matters such as past performance concerning safety or environmental compliance.

IV. APPLICATION OF PAST PERFORMANCE

A. Past Performance as an Indicator of Future Performance

As stated above, past performance is the key factor in determining the level of confidence that the Government should place in an offeror's promises. There is great intuitive appeal to the idea that the Government should evaluate an offeror's record of performance as part of the process of evaluating competing offerors during the source selection process. After all, most people would agree that a good performer is more likely to deliver a satisfactory product or service than a poor performer.

This notion of the predictive value of the past is deeply embedded in our culture and is reflected in all kinds of evaluations. Colleges consider a prospective student's high school grade point average to be somewhat indicative of collegiate academic performance. Businesspeople ask prospective employees to identify their previous employers. People looking for a contractor to remodel their homes ask for references.

This is not to say that history is destiny. Nearly everyone knows or has heard of poor students who became great scholars and of fine students who did not live up to their potential; cowards who became heroes and heroes who ran from danger; losers who became winners and winners who lost everything. The past may provide clues to the future, but few believe that it is entirely determinative.

Still, considering the past is one way to reduce uncertainty and risk when deciding on some future course of action. Thus, an employer who must choose between two prospective employees — one who performed well in the last job and one who performed poorly — will probably consider the employee who performed well to be the better bet, and the other to be more of a risk.

B. Source Selection "Risk" Assessments

The FAR and some agency FAR supplements use the term "risk." For example, FAR 15.612(d)(2), addressing formal source selection documentation, includes the following sentence:

> The supporting documentation prepared for the selection decision shall show the relative differences among proposals and their strengths, weaknesses, and risks in terms of the evaluation factors.

The underlying concept of risk has two elements. The first element is a calculation or estimate of the probability of the occurrence of a specified event. The second element is a measure of the consequences that would follow from the occurrence of that event.[54]

As used in the context of source selection, the word "risk" seems to connote probability of success or failure. Consider, for example, the following definitions of risk in AFFARS Appendix AA:

> High [Risk] — Significant doubt exists, based on the offeror's performance record, that the offeror can perform the proposed effort;
>
> Moderate [Risk] — Some doubt exists, based on the offeror's performance record, that the offeror can perform the proposed effort;
>
> Low [Risk] — Little doubt exists, based on the offeror's proposed record, that the offeror can perform the proposed effort; and

---

[54] John Raftery, *Risk Analysis in Project Management* (1994), pp. 5-8.

Not Applicable — No significant performance record is identifiable.[55]

The event contemplated in these definitions is not well defined, but seems to be a complete failure to perform. Presumably, the consequences of a complete failure would be more or less catastrophic to the agency. But a complete failure to perform is extremely unlikely. Very few contractors fail completely — so few, in fact, that one must wonder about the meaning and usefulness of these definitions as expressions of risk.

These definitions are really expressions of varying degrees of confidence that the offeror will satisfy the agency.   There is no calculation of consequences, which is a normal component of even informal expressions of risk. (For example, "If you jump out of the window you will (probably) break your neck.") In the Air Force regulation "low" risk simply means "we have a high level of confidence that if we select this offeror we will be satisfied with the results." "High" risk means "we have little confidence that this offeror will produce satisfactory results."

The terms "risk" and "probability" are formal, technical concepts. Formal risk assessments and determinations of probability that conform to Bayesian rules of inference require a degree of statistical sophistication and procedural know-how. To measure risk in any meaningful way the risky event must be specified unambiguously and the probability and consequences of its occurrence known or estimated.[56]

But there is no probability for a unique event, such as the successful performance of a contract.   And while formal techniques exist for the development of less rigorous measures of expectation, even these entail a remarkable degree of analytical sophistication. Unless everyone involved understands that the term "risk" is being used informally, the results of an evaluation could be confusing and lead to criticism. To avoid confusion — and criticism from statisticians, decision analysts, and other professionals — this monograph uses (and encourages the adoption of) the term Level of Confidence Assessment Rating (LOCAR) instead of "risk assessment."   A

---

[55] *Formal Source Selection for Major Acquisitions*, AFFARS Appendix AA, § 305 (AFAC 29-33, Nov. 1, 1993).

[56] von Winterfeldt and Edwards, *supra* note 43, pp. 90-136.

level of confidence assessment is a judgment about how much confidence —
trust or reliance — an agency has in an offeror's promises.[57]

A level of confidence assessment may be expressed in numbers or
words, as described in Section II.D. Past performance need not be the only
element the Government uses to assess confidence.   However, past
performance should always be the key element in an agency's assessment.

The LOCAR is not a judgment about the offeror's past performance, but
rather an expression of the Government's reaction to the offeror's past
performance.   In order to develop LOCARs the Government must first
research each offeror's past, then rate each offeror's past performance, and
finally determine its own level of confidence in each offeror based on that
past performance rating. This approach, in which past performance is used
as an element of a level of confidence (risk) assessment, is consistent with
the requirements of OFPP Policy Letter No. 92-5.

V. RESEARCHING OFFEROR PAST PERFORMANCE

A. Finding Sources of Information

The agency should manage its assessment of each offeror's past
performance as a thorough investigation of the offeror's past. The objective
should be to develop a portfolio about the offeror that will inform the source
selection decision maker about the kind of business partner the offeror would
be if selected for contract award. The portfolio should be as complete and
informative as is reasonably possible.   FAR 15.608(a)(2)(i) contains the
following guidance:

---

[57] The LOCAR is simply an assessment of the probability of the event that
the offeror will keep its promises sufficiently to satisfy the customer. It is
different from a risk assessment mainly in that it includes no calculation of
consequences. Since each instance of contract performance is a more or less a
unique event, the relative frequency and classical methods (assumed symmetry
based on logical argument) of probability assessment are inapplicable. This
monograph makes no attempt to justify the use of subjective probability
assessments, but those readers who would like a complete theoretical justification
should consult von Winterfeldt and Edwards, *supra* note 43, pp. 90-136.

The number and severity of an offeror's problems, the effectiveness of corrective actions taken, the offeror's overall work record, and the age and relevance of past performance information should be considered at the time it is used.

FAR 15.608(a)(2)(ii) provides as follows:

Where past performance is to be evaluated, the solicitation shall afford offerors the opportunity to identify Federal, state and local government, and private contracts performed by the offerors that were similar in nature to the contract being evaluated, so that the Government may verify the offerors' past performance on these contracts. In addition, at the discretion of the contracting officer, the offerors may provide information on problems encountered on the identified contracts and the offerors' corrective actions. Past performance information may also be obtained from other sources known to the Government. The source and type of past performance information to be included in the evaluation is within the broad discretion of agency acquisition officials and should be tailored to the circumstances of each acquisition. Evaluations of contractor performance prepared in accordance with 48 CFR part 42, subpart 42.15 are one source of performance information which may be used.

Unless Government personnel have had direct experience with a company, the only way they can rate that company's past performance is to obtain information from others. Sources of information are persons who have made or possess records of observations of an offeror's business conduct. They include former and present customers, former and present subcontractors, Government agencies, business associations, and public interest groups.

One way to find sources of information is to ask each offeror to provide a list of former and present customers and subcontractors during some period of time, i.e., a five-year period. The offeror should certify that the list is complete and accurate.

An experience/past performance matrix of the type in Figure 2 below provides a useful format for obtaining references from competing offerors. Agencies can prepare the matrix as a form and attach it to the RFP for the offerors' use. It is a convenient method for obtaining a list of references, associating each reference with specific work of the prospective contract, making a preliminary assessment of the breadth and depth of an offeror's experience with that work, and comparing offerors on the basis of the breadth and depth of their experience.

The first column in the table is for references. (The example illustrates a complete entry in the first row only.) The remaining columns are headed by the contract statement of work or specification work elements. The agency should instruct offerors to insert information (name, address, point(s) of contact, and telephone number) about their references (one reference for each contract performed for a customer) in the reference column, at the beginning of each row of the matrix. The agency should instruct offerors to indicate what work they did for the reference by inserting a "P" or an "S" in the row cells to the right of the reference entry. A "P" indicates that the offeror was a prime contractor; the "S" indicates that it was a subcontractor. A subscript should be included for each subcontract entry to indicate the subcontract tier.

References	Contract Statement of Work/ Specification Work Elements					
	3.1.1	3.1.2	3.2.1	3.2.2	3.3.1	3.3.2
ABC Corp. (Address) (POC) (Tel. No.)	S_2			S_2		
USAF	P	P	P		P	P
Brown, Inc.	S_1	S_1			S_1	
EPA		P			P	
FAA			P	P		

Figure 2. *Experience/Past Performance Matrix*

The agency should further instruct offerors to provide a list of all their first tier subcontractors for each prime contract reference entry, and the name of their customer's customer for each subcontract reference entry. The agency should also provide a form for offerors to provide more extensive information about the reference work, such as: date of award, price or cost, period of performance, descriptions of supplies delivered or services rendered, and information about litigation. This form should be submitted with the completed experience/past performance matrix.

It seems a dubious proposition to ask offerors to assess the relevance of their own experience or the effectiveness of their own solutions to performance problems, given that they will likely cast everything in the most favorable light. A better approach is to ask the references for their opinions about the offeror's performance and then, if the agency conducts discussions, provide offerors with the opportunity to respond to unfavorable opinions from references, as required by FAR 15.610(c)(6).

Although FAR 15.608 addresses past performance in terms of "relevance" and "similar in nature," it would be a mistake to limit the assessment of an offeror's past performance to those contracts in which the offeror performed work similar to that to be performed under the prospective contract. One of the objectives in evaluating past performance should be to determine whether or not the offeror is a well-managed firm and whether or not it would make a trustworthy business partner. Thus, the investigation should not be excessively work-specific.

Any assessment of past performance should include an analysis of financial statements. Financial statements are important sources of information about the past performance of an offeror's managers. Consideration of financial status and trends are standard elements of the evaluation of past performance in the commercial sector Consider the following statements from the chapters on supplier evaluation in the two most widely used textbooks about commercial purchasing:

> Presumably, financial stability and strength are indicators of good management and competitive ability. Financial statements, therefore, are a reasonable source of information about a supplier's past performance. Whether the vendor will continue to perform in the same manner in the future is an assessment the purchaser must make, taking all available information, including the financial side, into account.[58]

---

[58]   Leenders, et al., *supra* note 16, p. 256.

In addition to informing a buyer about a supplier's capability to perform a contract, financial information can be useful in other ways as well. Financially strong firms are usually managerially strong; hence, they generally make good suppliers. An analysis of a firm's balance sheet and operating statement is helpful to a buyer in many ways.[59]

No Government agency should enter into an important business relationship without first investigating its prospective partner's past financial performance. It must be emphasized that the purpose of this review of financial statements is to assess general managerial performance on the basis of financial performance as an element of overall past performance. As such it is part of the comparative assessment of past performance, as described in FAR 15.608(a)(2). The review is not for the purpose of determining financial capacity, i.e., financial responsibility, as described in FAR Subpart 9.1.

Agencies should require competing offerors to submit financial statements for each of their last three complete fiscal years. Such statements should include, as a minimum, balance sheets (statements of financial position) and statements of profit and loss (statement of net income). These should be reviewed to determine whether the firm's financial performance reflects stability and strength or instability and weakness.   Financial statements should be audited or at least reviewed by an independent auditor. Some offerors may complain about the expense of obtaining an audit. Agencies should evaluate such complaints in light of the size, duration, and potential profitability of the prospective contract. Agencies may want to consider tax returns as a substitute for financial statements.

An agency should also obtain a complete list of an offeror's former Government customers from the Federal Procurement Data System (FPDS), which is managed by the General Services Administration. With few exceptions, agencies must report contract awards in excess of $25,000 to the FPDS on SF 279 or DD Form 350. The FPDS will provide a list of a company's Government contracts back to fiscal year 1976. The address and telephone number of the FPDS is in FAR Part 4.

---

[59] Dobler, et al., *supra* note 16, p. 197.

Agencies may want to search legal databases such as LEXIS and WESTLAW for information about litigation in which a company has been involved. They could also check the index of publications such as *Federal Contracts Report* and *Government Contracts Reports*. State, county, and municipal licensing and law enforcement agencies may also have information about a company's business conduct. If a company's stock is publicly traded, the public library may have useful information such as financial reports. Other sources of information include newspapers, consumer protection organizations, and better business bureaus.

B. Obtaining Reliable Past Performance Information

Evaluating past performance is a type of market survey research project. Researchers must collect, sort, and collate the information, make judgments, and assign ratings. The most difficult phase of the work is the collection of information, because researchers must locate and question sources of information, either in person, by telephone, or in writing. Because this work can consume so much time, it is probably best for an agency to establish a team of persons who will be entirely devoted to these tasks during the source selection, especially if the agency anticipates receiving a large number of proposals.

The Government should determine the size of the team primarily on the basis of the anticipated number of offerors. A team leader should be appointed if the team includes three or more persons. Among the key qualifications for team membership should be the ability to obtain information by formulating intelligent, pertinent questions, and the ability to listen carefully and to pursue leads. These inquiries are not police interrogations, and interviewers should put sources of information at ease while drawing out information.

The team members should decide how they will collect information prior to the receipt of proposals. There are basically four ways to do this: (1) face-to-face interviews, (2) mailed questionnaires, (3) telephone interviews, or (4) some combination of the three. Face-to-face interviews are optimal, but travel usually makes them too costly and time-consuming. Mailed questionnaires can be very effective, but sources of information may not respond in a timely fashion, if at all. Therefore, telephone interviews are usually the most practical way to collect past performance information for most source selections.

In order to ensure that pertinent information is obtained, the past performance team should prepare a list of standard questions to ask sources of information in given categories — former and present customers, subcontractors, and so forth. The questions should reflect the evaluation rating system standards and the rating scale definitions that will be used to assess an offeror's strengths and weaknesses.

Agencies should exercise care when developing questionnaires. In a 1995 protest decision involving an Air Force information resources acquisition, the General Services Administration Board of Contract Appeals (GSBCA) took note of testimony by one of the protester's expert witnesses that the Air Force's survey procedure with regard to past performance was "not very scientific" and that many of the questions on the Air Force's questionnaire were poorly worded. Although the GSBCA concluded that the Air Force's findings about the protester's past performance were valid, the board warned that the process used by the Air Force to assess past performance "may not be reliable enough to withstand challenges in all cases."[60]   This is a clear warning that agencies should develop past performance survey questionnaires on the basis of sound principles of survey research.[61]

Interviewers should make an appointment to conduct an interview, rather than telephoning potential sources of information unannounced, thereby catching them unprepared. The prospective interviewee should also be informed as to how much time will be needed. A suggested time frame for the interview is one hour. If possible, the agency should mail or fax the questions to the interviewee in advance of the appointment. This allows the interviewee adequate time to prepare. Tape recording is discouraged because

---

[60] *Unisys Corp. v. Department of the Air Force*, GSBCA 13129-P, 1995 GSBCA LEXIS (March 3, 1995).

[61] For descriptions of how to develop survey questionnaires, see Earl Babbie, *Survey Research Methods* (1973; 2d ed., 1990); Linda A. Suskie, *Questionnaire Survey Research: What Works* (1992); and U.S. General Accounting Office, *Developing and Using Questionnaires* (1986).

it may have a chilling effect on the process. Interviewers should take copious notes to ensure that all information is captured.

Interviewers should avoid group interviews because people behave and express themselves differently in groups than in one-on-one interviews. For instance, some people retire from group discussion and withhold their opinions, while others may dominate the discussion. Although there are benefits to group interviews — people spur each other's memory, and extreme opinions are challenged by others in the group — one-on-one interviews are probably better for the capture of frank opinions. In the same vein, being interviewed by a group of anonymous people on a speakerphone can be daunting to some sources of information, and they may end up reluctant to express any opinion.

The interviewer should be well organized and efficient when conducting the interview so as not to waste the interviewee's time. The interviewer should introduce himself or herself, identify his or her organization, provide a brief description of the procurement, and explain what the interview will cover and how the information will be used. The interviewer should not promise anonymity or confidentiality to the interviewee, since a protester may be able to force the agency to reveal the interviewee's identity through legal procedures.

The interviewer should begin with simple questions such as the place and time period of the offeror's past performance, the nature of the work involved, and the past and present relationship with the offeror. The interviewer should gradually build up to more complex questions that require the interviewee to make judgments. This approach allows the interviewee to gain confidence and spurs recollection.

Just prior to the end of the interview, the interviewer should ask the interviewee for a summary opinion, and then offer some word options. The following are sample questions:

- In summary, which of the following would you choose to describe the quality of Company X's service: "significantly better than acceptable," "slightly better than acceptable," "acceptable," "slightly less than acceptable," or "entirely unacceptable"?

or

- In summary, which of the following would you choose to describe Company X's willingness to cooperate to resolve performance disagreements: "highly cooperative," "cooperative," "somewhat uncooperative," or "highly uncooperative"?

A slightly different approach would be to offer the interviewee a proposition and then ask to what degree he or she agrees or disagrees with it. For example, the interviewer might ask: "Which of the following expressions would you choose to describe your reaction to the following statement, 'Company X is a reliable contractor': 'agree completely,' 'agree significantly,' 'agree slightly,' 'disagree slightly,' 'disagree significantly,' or 'disagree completely'?"

When asking questions of this kind, the members of the past performance team should agree on what word choices to offer interviewees and should offer the same word choices to all interviewees. In this way responses can be counted and statistically analyzed.

Interviewers should ensure that questions are worded so that interviewees understand precisely what they are being asked to describe. For instance, in the first sample question the word "quality" is vague. It could mean very different things to different people; the interviewees' responses, therefore, could mean very different things. What may seem to be diverse responses to a single question could really be responses to different questions. A better-worded question would be more specific: "Which of the following would you choose to characterize the thoroughness with which Company X conformed to the technical standards in the statement of work: 'painstakingly thorough,' 'acceptably thorough,' 'superficial,' or 'careless'?"

Every interview should end with a request for the names and telephone numbers of three other persons who have had experience with the offeror under study. These leads should be followed up until the past performance team believes it has enough information to form the basis for a sound judgment.

C. Documenting the Research

Interviewers should complete an interview report immediately following each interview. This report should include the date, time, and duration of the interview; the interviewee's location; and whether the interview was face-to-face or telephonic. The interviewee should be identified by name and job title, with a complete mailing address and telephone number. The report should summarize the interview and state whether the overall comments reflected favorably or unfavorably on the offeror. A copy of the interview questionnaire and interview notes should be attached to the report. When all interviews are completed, the information should be summarized into categories of strengths and weaknesses. The interview reports, attached interview questionnaires, and interview notes should be the documentary basis for assigning past performance ratings.

VI. RATING OFFEROR PAST PERFORMANCE

A. General Rating Techniques

After the past performance team finishes its research, the next step is to rate the offerors' past performance. Rating is the process of judging how good or bad each offeror's past performance was, based on the information gathered by the past performance team. This rating is used to determine how much confidence the agency should place in the offeror's promises.

In order to rate an offeror's past performance, the Government should develop a rating scale. The scale should reflect the idea that past performance can take any value along a range, from good to bad. By developing a scale that describes different degrees of quality, the agency can focus its thinking about the specific performance of each offeror.

The development of a scale of past performance is challenging but not impossible. The scale must describe varying degrees of past performance quality. A simple descriptive scale follows:

- Entirely favorable past performance
- More favorable than unfavorable past performance
- No record of past performance or inconclusive record

- More unfavorable than favorable past performance
- Entirely unfavorable past performance

An adjective can be assigned to each of these categories as a label, as follows:

Excellent — Entirely favorable past performance
Good — More favorable than unfavorable past performance
None — No record of past performance or inconclusive record
Marginal — More unfavorable than favorable past performance
Poor — Entirely unfavorable past performance

Instead of adjectives, numbers can be assigned as follows:

(+2) —   Entirely favorable past performance
(+1) —   More favorable than unfavorable past performance
(0) —   No record of past performance or inconclusive record
(-1) —   More unfavorable than favorable past performance
(-2) —   Entirely unfavorable past performance

Both adjectives and numbers are category labels. They serve the same purpose as academic letter grades — to provide a convenient, brief, summary expression of more complicated ideas. Numbers do not represent actual quantities of anything and do not make ratings more "objective" or precise. The main advantage of numbers over adjectives is that they are less awkward to work with when evaluators want to use more than four or five rating categories. Within reason, the more rating categories available to the evaluators, whether numerical, adjectival, or color-coded, the easier it is to make fine distinctions among offerors and thereby determine which offeror is best.

The more detailed the rating definitions the greater the likelihood that evaluators will conform to the same scale. More detailed descriptions improve an adjectival rating system. For example, the five adjectives used above could be defined as follows:

Excellent — A significant majority of the sources of information are consistently firm in stating that the offeror's performance was superior and that they would unhesitatingly do business with the offeror again.

Complaints are negligible or unfounded. The offeror has no record of criminal conduct, civil fraud, or negligence, or the record is old and the offeror has demonstrated by more recent performance that corrective action has made the likelihood of such conduct in the future highly improbable.

Good — Most sources of information state that the offeror's performance was good, better than average, etc., and that they would willingly do business with the offeror again. Complaints, though perhaps well-founded, are few and relatively minor. The offeror has no record of criminal conduct, civil fraud, or negligence, or the record is old and the offeror has demonstrated by more recent performance that corrective action has made the likelihood of such conduct in the future highly improbable.

None — No record exists, or sources of information are roughly divided over the quality of the offeror's performance. While some state that they would do business with the offeror again, others are doubtful or would not. Complaints are balanced by reports of good work. The offeror has no record of criminal conduct, civil fraud, or negligence, or the record is old.

Marginal — Many sources of information make unfavorable reports about the offeror's performance and either express serious doubts about doing business with the offeror again or state that they would refuse to do so. However, there are some favorable reports, and some sources of information indicate that they would do business with the offeror again. There are many significant, serious, and well-founded complaints, but there are some reports of very good performance. The offeror may have been indicted, pled guilty, or may have been found guilty in matters of criminal conduct, but the issues are unresolved, relatively minor, or do not reflect a company-wide or managerial pattern of wrongdoing. The offeror may have lost civil suits for fraud or negligence, but there is no company-wide or managerial pattern of fraudulent, negligent, or criminal conduct.

Poor — A significant majority of sources of information are consistently firm in stating that the offeror's performance was entirely unsatisfactory and that they would not do business with the offeror again under any circumstances. Customer complaints are substantial or numerous and are well-founded. Or, although not debarred or suspended, the offeror is under indictment or has been convicted of criminal conduct, or has been found civilly liable for fraud or negligence. The offeror either has presented no persuasive evidence of having taken appropriate corrective action that will guard against such conduct in the foreseeable future, or it appears unlikely that the corrective action will be effective.

Words should be chosen with care. It is not necessary, and probably not possible, to achieve mathematical precision. Remember that while the reason for defining the points on the scale is to increase the degree of coherence among evaluators, the scale will be used to describe subjective assessments that are unavoidably fuzzy around the edges. Any attempt to define the scale points with mathematical precision will involve excessive exposition and will likely fail anyway.

B. Rating the New Offeror with No Past Performance

There is some concern over the evaluation of past performance as part of source selection on the ground that it is potentially unfair to new companies that have not established a record. OFPP Policy Letter No. 92-5, which was the first expression of policy with regard to past performance, stated that Government policy was to "[a]llow newly established firms to compete for contracts even though they lack a history of past performance." Section 1091(b)(2) of the FASA states:

> In the case of an offeror with respect to which there is no information on past contract performance or with respect to which information on past contract performance is not available, the offeror may not be evaluated favorably or unfavorably on the factor of past performance.

FAR 15.608(a)(2)(iii) states, "Firms lacking relevant past performance history shall receive a neutral evaluation for past performance." Two questions emerge: (1) What does "neutral" mean in this context? and (2) How does one implement the neutrality policy?

Consider the following scenario: An agency is evaluating offerors for the award of a service contract. The agency is using only two evaluation factors: past performance and price. The agency receives two offers:

	Agency Rating	Contract Price
Offeror A	Excellent past performance	$1,000,000
Offeror B	New company; no past performance record	$1,000,000

Figure 3. *Sample Evaluation Factors*

Assuming that the proposed prices are realistic and reasonable, very few people would pick Offeror B, which represents a higher risk than Offeror A, with no offsetting benefit to make the risk worth taking. But if Offeror A's price were significantly higher than Offeror B's price, some people might be willing to take a chance on Offeror B in exchange for the savings. In other words, they would trade off the confidence they have in Offeror A due to its excellent past performance in exchange for the savings offered by Offeror B. (Different people would require different levels of marginal savings before they would make the switch from A to B.)[62]

The new firm is at a disadvantage because most people reasonably perceive it to represent a higher risk. If the proposition that past performance is often indicative of future performance is valid, then it is reasonable to argue that the absence of a record of past performance is a reasonable basis for doubts about what to expect from a company in the future. The source selection authority would be justified, therefore, in considering award to the new firm to be riskier than award to the firm with an excellent record. It also seems reasonable to take such uncertainty into account when making source selection decisions. In order to overcome that disadvantage, the new firm would have to offer a worthwhile tradeoff. It is not inherently unfair to consider the lack of a performance record to be a basis for uncertainty or to take such uncertainty into consideration when making the source selection decision. Indeed, it is common sense to do so.

---

[62] The author has informally polled his seminar students based on this scenario on countless occasions. These unscientific experiments have always verified a general preference for the experienced offeror with excellent past performance over the offeror with no performance record.

The question is: Would doing so be consistent with FAR 15.608(a)(2)(iii)? Would a "neutral" evaluation effectively require that the agency eliminate past performance as an evaluation factor?   The specific intent of the "neutral" rule is unclear.

The OFPP has issued a description of a set of "best practices" for the evaluation of past performance. These include the suggestion that agencies give new firms a score for past performance that is the "average" of the scores of the other competing offerors. This suggestion has no merit. From the point of view of the decision maker, the most important fact is that the reason the new firm has no record is that the firm has no experience with the work. It would be arbitrary to assign it a score based on the average of the scores given to the other competitors. In addition to being arbitrary, it could violate the FASA provision against favorable or unfavorable evaluation based on past performance. Worse, it would hide from the decision maker the fact that the offeror has no experience.

One approach to the problem posed by FAR 15.608(a)(2)(iii) may be to distinguish the evaluation of past performance from the use of the evaluation when making the source selection decision. Under this approach the score assigned for no past performance must be "neutral" or "none" rather than "poor;" nevertheless, the decision maker could consider that score to be disadvantageous in comparison to a score of "excellent" or "good." However, because the specific intent of the policy is unclear, it is also unclear whether this approach would be acceptable in the event of a protest to the Comptroller General or the GSBCA.

A different approach would be to handle a new firm's lack of experience as just that — a lack of experience. This would require the use of experience as a separate evaluation factor. The new firm would be scored "neutral" for past performance, but given an unfavorable score for experience. This, too, however, could be deemed to be inconsistent with the spirit of FAR 15.608(a)(2)(iii).

How should the Government rate the firm with no past performance? The answer is that the new firm should be given a rating of "none" (or 0 on the numerical scale described above). This would accurately reflect the firm's history. How that rating should be translated into a LOCAR is described in Section VII below.

Some individuals have proposed that the Government should rate new companies on the basis of the experience and past performance of their managers and other key personnel and on the experience and past performance of its subcontractors. This is the position of the Comptroller General. However, this assumes that the experiences and successes of individual members of a new organization will ensure the success of that organization, but this is not necessarily true. Consider a football game in which a team made up of the best players from different teams, players who have never played together, plays against the previous year's Super Bowl winner. How many people would wager against the Super Bowl winner? Do the skills of the individual players on the new team contribute something to its capabilities? Of course they do. Is that team likely to be as effective as the team that has played together and proven itself to be a winner? Of course not.

Similarly, subcontractors must work within the context of the totality of the contracting complex. Their ability to translate their experience and past performance into successful future performance depends in no small measure on the ability of the prime contractor to manage the integration of subcontracted and in-house effort. A new and inexperienced prime contractor organization may make it difficult for subcontractors to succeed. Many are the large programs that have suffered because of the failure to successfully integrate the work of subcontractors.

When assessing level of confidence in the ability and willingness of an offeror to keep its promises, the Government should consider all relevant factors, including the qualifications of key personnel and subcontractors. But past performance is about the history of the offeror as an organization. Organizations have existences that transcend individual employees and managers and subcontract relationships, and the experiences and successes of individuals and subcontractors do not necessarily add up to organizational success. The qualifications of key individual employees and subcontractors should be separately considered, if relevant, but they should not be used to offset the advantage enjoyed by companies that have demonstrated their effectiveness as organizations.

VII. DEVELOPING A LOCAR

A. Defining the Level of Confidence Assessment

An agency's LOCAR of an offeror (a risk assessment) is an adjustment factor, and is applied to the agency's assessment of the offeror's promised value in order to determine its expected value. A LOCAR of 1 (complete confidence) indicates that the agency has complete confidence in an offeror. A LOCAR of 0 (no confidence) indicates that the agency has no confidence in an offeror. A LOCAR of .5 means that the agency is unsure — neither confident nor lacking confidence.

The evaluators' assessment of an offer tells the Government's decision maker how much an offeror's promises would be worth if the offeror kept its promises. The expected value rating tells the source selection authority what the evaluators think an offeror's promises are actually worth, based on their assessment of both the offer and the offeror's ability and willingness to keep its promises. If the evaluators assign a LOCAR of 1, indicating that they are entirely confident in an offeror's promises, then the offeror's expected value will be the same as its promised value. If the evaluators are entirely *not* confident in an offeror, then the offeror's expected value will be 0. If the evaluators are unsure about the offeror, then the offeror's expected value will be one-half of its promised value, and so forth.

B. Developing the LOCAR Scale

In order to rate levels of confidence in competing offerors, an agency should develop a LOCAR scale, which is a set of scoring rules. A LOCAR scale should include a range of values from 0 through 1, with equal decimal intervals of .1 between the two extremes. If past performance is the only LOCAR factor, then the LOCAR scale should be keyed to the past performance rating scale (see Section VI). If other factors are to be included, such as financial condition, then the scale must include references to the rating scales for those factors.

Assume that an agency decides to base its LOCAR on offerors' records of past performance and on their financial condition. The agency should establish its rating scale by beginning with the end points of 0 and 1. The agency could define these points as follows:

0 — Completely Not Confident. The offeror received an extremely low rating (-2) for past performance, based on almost entirely unfavorable reports of past performance. The offeror has recently filed for bankruptcy, or analyses of standard liquidity, activity, debt, and profitability ratios indicate that the offeror is on the brink of bankruptcy. The offeror's financial resources fall far short of the requirements of the prospective contract.

1 — Completely Confident. The offeror received the highest possible rating (+2) for past performance, based on entirely favorable reports of past performance. Based on analyses of standard liquidity, activity, debt, and profitability ratios, the offeror has been found to be in the best possible financial condition. The offeror's financial resources far exceed the requirements of the prospective contract.

Next, the agency could define the LOCAR scale midpoint of .5 as follows:

.5 — Neutral. The offeror's record of past performance was neither predominantly favorable nor unfavorable. Standard financial analyses indicate that while the offeror's condition is presently stable, and neither especially strong nor weak, its condition could improve or deteriorate dramatically, depending on the outcome of certain ongoing contracts or in-house projects. It is unclear whether the offeror will have financial resources that will be adequate to meet the requirements of the prospective contract.

Having defined the extremes and the midpoint of confidence, it is not necessary to define the intermediate points in great detail. The evaluators can decide on an assignment of points anywhere along the scale through discussion and debate among themselves. The literature on probability assessment and risk analysis describes a wide variety of techniques, but all are ultimately designed to elicit subjective assessments. One pair of highly respected experts urge the use of any technique that promotes "hard thinking and insight."[63] They have the following to say about all such assessments:

> [T]hose who elicit probabilities or other measures of uncertainty are blessed in one way. No probability assessment (except 0 or 1) can be shown to be wrong directly. Methods for showing that such numbers are biased or inappropriate do exist but are tedious, contentious, inapplicable to single instances or small ensembles, and rather rarely used.[64]

The LOCAR ratings should not be thought of as precise descriptions but rather as judgments. The LOCAR ratings are not formal probabilities, nor are they assessments of risk in the technical sense of that term. They are subjective expressions of the evaluators' collective level of confidence -- i.e., belief, trust or reliance — in the competing offerors.

Evaluators should determine their collective level of confidence through free-form discussion and debate. The LOCAR should reflect a consensus. Majority rule and averaging of individual numerical ratings are poor substitutes for thoughtful discussion and intellectual give-and-take. However, for this approach to be effective, the team members should be chosen for their qualities of reasonableness and the ability to express themselves thoughtfully.

The preceding exposition described a LOCAR scale as a scale of numbers. But those agencies that do not use numerical scoring may express the LOCAR adjectivally. Instead of numbers, the agency may use rating labels such as "completely confident," "mostly confident," "somewhat confident," "neutral," etc., or "high," "moderate," or "low." Of course, adjectival ratings do not permit the agency to calculate an expected value rating for the offerors. Instead, the agency would have to make an intuitive determination of expected value.

What about new companies? Their past performance rating should be 0 or "none," as indicated in Section VI. But what kind of LOCAR should they receive? The answer depends on whether or not past performance is the

---

[63] von Winterfeldt and Edwards, *supra* note 43, p. 114.

[64] *Id.*, p. 112.

only LOCAR element and on the nature of the contract work. If past performance is the only LOCAR factor and if the offeror has no organizational experience or record of successful organizational performance of any kind, then the answer depends on the nature of the contract work and the importance of organizational experience to a contractor's potential for success. If the work is complex and requires a high order of well-integrated organizational effort by a number of different functional groups, including subcontractors, then a company without any organizational experience or record of success should receive a LOCAR of less than .5. If, on the other hand, the work is simple and does not require a high order of integrated effort among functional groups, then it would be appropriate to give the new firm a LOCAR of .5.

If the LOCAR is based on past performance and other factors, then the LOCAR should depend on the new company's performance on those other factors and on those factors' relative importance to the LOCAR determination. Past performance should always be the most important factor in the LOCAR determination, but key personnel and subcontractor qualifications, financial condition, facility capacity, and other factors should, to some degree, offset, though not entirely compensate for, a lack of organizational experience and a history of successful performance. In these circumstances, a new firm with good ratings on other factors could conceivably receive a LOCAR of better than .5. In short, there is no reason to treat all new companies alike, without regard to the importance of experience to the likelihood of successful performance.

C. Applying the LOCAR to the Proposal Evaluation

The evaluation of a proposal results in (1) findings about the proposal's strengths, weaknesses, and deficiencies, and (2) a conclusion, based on the findings, about the relative worth of the proposal. These findings must be described in a report.[65]   Such reports are often referred to as "narratives."[66] They are often summarized in the form of a "score," which

---

[65]   FAR 15.608(a)(2) and 15.612(d)(2).

[66]   *See* Nash and Cibinic, *supra* note 49, pp. 350-352.

may take the form of a number, an adjective (such as "excellent," "very good," "good," "fair," "poor"), or a color code.[67]

These results, in whatever form they may take, indicate the value of what an offeror has promised to do or deliver. Thus, if an offeror's proposal is scored "very good," and if the Government awards the contract to that offeror, then the Government will receive "very good" value from that contractor if, and only if, that contractor keeps the promises that it made in its proposal. But will it keep those promises?

As described above, the LOCAR is an expression of the Government's degree of belief that the offeror will keep the promises that it made in its proposal. That belief is based on the offeror's past performance and on any other factors that the Government considered in determining its level of confidence in the offeror. The LOCAR is expressed either in numbers or words.

Once the Government has developed a LOCAR for each offer, it must apply them to the initial evaluations of the offerors' proposals in order to adjust those original conclusions, thereby determining the expected value of the proposals. The Government must reason from its original conclusion and its LOCAR to reach a new conclusion about the value of the competing proposals. If the original proposals were numerically scored and if the LOCAR is expressed in numerical form, then a mathematical calculation determines the expected value score (i.e., Original Value Score x LOCAR = Expected Value Score or 95 x .4 = 38). If the original value score and the LOCAR are valid expressions of the Government's findings, conclusions, and beliefs, then the expected value score will also be a valid expression.

If the Government's conclusions about the original scores and its levels of confidence are adjectivally expressed, then the Government cannot use the rules of arithmetic to develop an expected value score. An original score of "very good" cannot be multiplied by a LOCAR of "low confidence" to arrive at an expression of expected value. The Government will have to make an intuitive assessment of the expected value of the proposals. One solution

---

[67] *Id.*, pp. 346-350.

may be to develop rules of thumb. For example, the Government could develop a rule of thumb that provides as follows:

> An "excellent" proposal and a "high" level of confidence will result in an "excellent" expected value; an "excellent" proposal and a "moderate" level of confidence will be considered a "very good" proposal; and an "excellent" proposal and a "low" level of confidence will be considered a "good" proposal.

If the Government's evaluators find this approach to be excessively mechanical, they should develop a more flexible approach, such as free-form round-table discussion or Delphi-style techniques .

An important point: the application of the LOCAR should never result in an improvement in the original (promised value) proposal evaluation conclusion or score. The LOCAR is a type of probability assessment; the best LOCAR an offeror can receive is a numerical score of 1 or an adjectival expression such as "complete confidence." This being the case, the best expected value score that the Government should assign to an offeror is one that indicates that the Government can expect to receive value from the offeror that is equal to the value promised. Any LOCAR of less than 1 (or "complete confidence") will result in an expected value that is less than the promised value.

D. Describing LOCAR Procedure in RFPs

The FAR requires that the Government describe the evaluation factors for award and their relative importance in the RFP.[68] The Government must explain how it will use past performance and the LOCAR to make the source selection. The following language is recommended for inclusion in the RFP to explain the evaluation of past performance and the development and application of the LOCAR:

---

[68] FAR 15.605(e).

Evaluation Factors for Award.

The Government will award the contract to the offeror who represents the best overall expected value. In determining which offeror represents the best overall expected value, the Government will consider the following factors:

Proposal Evaluation Factors.

[The RFP should first describe the factors that will be applied to the evaluation of the proposals.]

Level of Confidence Assessment Rating.

The Government will develop a level of confidence assessment rating for each offeror. This rating will reflect the Government's degree of confidence that the offeror will keep the promises it made in its proposal. The rating will be used to adjust the Government's evaluation of the offeror's proposal, and may be highly influential to the determination of which offeror represents the best overall expected value.

The Government will consider the following factors when developing the level of confidence assessment rating:

Past performance. The offeror's record of past performance and experience, or the lack thereof, will be the most important factor in the development of the level of confidence assessment rating. The Government will evaluate the offeror's reputation for conforming to specifications and to standards of good workmanship, for accurately estimating and controlling costs, for adherence to contract schedules (including the administrative aspects of performance), for reasonable and cooperative behavior and commitment to customer satisfaction, and for having a businesslike concern for the interests of the customer. The Government will also evaluate the depth, breadth, relevance, and currency of the offeror's work experience.

[Describe any other factors that will be considered in developing the LOCAR, such as key personnel and subcontractor qualifications, financial condition, capacity and condition of facilities and equipment, etc.]

This language fulfills the FAR requirement to describe how the Government will use past performance and the LOCAR to make the source selection decision.

VIII. DOCUMENTING EVALUATION RESULTS AND CONDUCTING DISCUSSIONS

A. Documenting Evaluation Results

Once the evaluations of past performance have been completed, the evaluators must document their findings and judgments. The documentation should be in the form of a written report. The report should describe to the source selection authority the evaluators' collective summary judgment about the quality of each offeror's past performance and the bases for that judgment. The past performance research reports (described above) should be included in an appendix.

The evaluators' collective summary judgment may be expressed in the form of a table of numerical or adjectival ratings, or expository prose. These should be supported by or include descriptions of the evaluators' analyses and evaluation of the offerors' strengths and weaknesses, as identified during the past performance survey interviews. Figure 4 below shows an outline for the report.

This report should be succinct. The introduction should briefly identify the evaluation team members, then describe the past performance survey research process. The process should not be described in excruciating detail, but merely provide an overview, including a description of the schedule of key events and the identity of the competing offerors. Finally, the factors that were used to develop the LOCAR and the method used to rate those factors should be described.

LEVEL OF CONFIDENCE ASSESSMENT RATING
(LOCAR) REPORT

I. Introduction
    A. Identity of team members
    B. Team research activities
    C. Identity of offerors
    D. LOCAR factors

II. Offerors' past performance ratings

III. Offerors' LOCARs

IV. Attachments
    A. Research reports
    B. Rating worksheets

Figure 4. *LOCAR Report Outline*

The second section of the report should briefly summarize the results of the past performance evaluation by stating each offeror's rating and the rationale. The third section should state each offeror's LOCAR and the rationale. The amount of detail is somewhat offeror-dependent, but it should reflect the interests and needs of the source selection authority. The information need not be exhaustive, but should include enough detail to allow the reader to be able to follow the evaluators' reasoning from findings through judgment. It is best to assume that, in the event of a protest, the protester will be able to obtain a copy of this report, so the presentation of facts, findings, and judgment should be made effectively and persuasively. The last section of the report should include all of the evaluators' research documentation and rating worksheets.

B. Conducting Discussions about Past Performance

While the FAR requires that agencies conduct discussions with all offerors in the competitive range, Comptroller General protest decisions seem to indicate that the Comptroller will not fault an agency for failing to reveal its findings that an offeror has a poor record of past performance.[69] The logic behind these decisions seems to be that an offeror's performance record is history and cannot be changed; findings of poor past performance, therefore, need not be revealed, since the purpose of discussions is to give offerors an opportunity to improve their proposals by eliminating weaknesses and deficiencies.

However, the problem with this logic is that the Government's evaluation of past performance is based on human observations and opinions, which may be erroneous or unfounded. Given an opportunity, an offeror may be able to prove that a damaging observation is in error or that an unfavorable opinion is unfounded, thereby improving the evaluation of its past performance.

The best practice is for the Government to reveal during discussions any damaging reports and unfavorable opinions about an offeror's past performance. It should give the offeror an opportunity to respond and then consider the response, if any, when making a final assessment of its level of confidence.

What should the Government do if it decides to make an award on the basis of initial proposals, without discussions? One argument is that the Government should not give offerors the chance to address damaging and unfavorable information about past performance, because such communications would constitute discussions. But another argument is that discussions are communications that pertain to the content of the proposal, and past performance information is not part of the proposal but rather information about the offeror. Thus, allowing offerors to respond to damaging and unfavorable reports would not constitute discussions.[70]

---

[69] For an analysis, see Carl Peckinpaugh, *Evaluations of Vendor Experience and Past Performance in Government Contracting Decisions*, 60 FCR 677 (Dec. 27, 1993).

[70] FAR 15.601 defines "discussions" as "any oral or written communication between the Government and an offeror (other than communications for the purpose of minor clarification), whether or not initiated by the Government, that (a) involves information essential for determining the acceptability of a proposal; or (b) provides the offeror an opportunity to revise or modify its proposal." Past

Offerors would not be allowed to revise their proposals, but only to respond to information about themselves. So long as all offerors are treated fairly and given an equal opportunity to respond to damaging and unfavorable reports, the Government should be allowed to exchange information about past performance without being required to conduct discussions about the proposals.[71]

IX. CONCLUSION

This monograph describes a relatively simple method of applying past performance to the evaluation of competitive proposals in the source selection process. It describes an approach in which past performance is used to develop an adjustment factor, called a Level of Confidence Assessment Rating or LOCAR, which is simply a type of probability assessment. That assessment is used to adjust the Government's conclusions about the value of the promises that offerors make in order to arrive at an assessment of the "true" or expected value of those promises.

This method, new only in its specific details, is nothing more than a greatly simplified version of techniques that form part of the body of multiple attribute decision analysis literature and that have been used for many years in a wide variety of applications. Much of the research that developed those techniques was Government-funded.[72]

The idea that observations and opinions about offerors' past performance should be considered in evaluating them during source selection has great intuitive appeal. A review of the protest decisions of the Comptroller General shows that agencies have evaluated past performance for many

---

performance does not affect the "acceptability" of a proposal, and a response to damaging or unfavorable information does not constitute a revision to an offeror's proposal because past performance is not something that an offeror *proposes* (i.e., promises).

[71] This argument is technical and subtle, and readers should not rely on it without legal advice.

[72] *See* von Winterfeldt and Edwards, *supra* note 43, for examples and an extensive bibliography.

years, and have generally prevailed in protests of their evaluations and their use of those evaluations in making source selection decisions.

In 1994 the Government launched a major campaign to apply past performance to the evaluation of competing offerors in all source selections over $100,000 and to develop a Government-wide past performance evaluation system. The Department of Defense implemented such a system in 1963 only to abandon it in 1971, declaring that "the benefits derived . . . were not sufficient to warrant the cost involved."[73] It is too soon to tell whether the new program will be able to avoid the failures of the old.

The most difficult problem confronting agencies that plan to evaluate past performance during source selection is finding enough reliable information to make an intelligent assessment of the quality of an offeror's past performance and to develop a rational level of confidence assessment. This far outweighs the problem of ensuring that Government evaluators use a rational approach to applying past performance in source selection. Protest decisions show that Government agencies are able to make defensible assessments and use them effectively when making source selection decisions.

---

[73] Revision 10 to ASPR, Nov. 30, 1971.